LOVE
AND
GRATITUDE

Reference Notes

The source for this pamphlet is Recording #615-2,
a Joel Goldsmith class from the
1951 First Seattle Series: Tape 2, side 2.
This recording is currently available in audiotape,
CD, or MP3 format at www.joelgoldsmith.com.

On page 117 of *The Spiritual Journey of Joel
Goldsmith*, Lorraine Sinkler explains the
origin of the pamphlet *Love and Gratitude*.

Other Titles in This Series

LOVE
AND
GRATITUDE

Joel S. Goldsmith

Acropolis Books, Publisher
Longboat Key, Florida

Love and Gratitude by Joel S. Goldsmith

From Chapters 12 and 13 of Collected Essays of Joel S. Goldsmith, © 1986 Thelma McDonald.

Acropolis Books, Inc.
Longboat Key, Florida
www.acropolisbooks.com

Except the Lord build the house,
they labour in vain that build it.

Psalm 127

Illumination dissolves all material ties and binds men together with the golden chains of spiritual understanding; it acknowledges only the leadership of the Christ; it has no ritual or rule but the divine, impersonal universal Love; no other worship than the inner Flame that is ever lit at the shrine of Spirit. This union is the free state of spiritual brotherhood. The only restraint is the discipline of Soul; therefore, we know liberty without license; we are a united universe without physical limits; a divine service to God without ceremony or creed. The illumined walk without fear – by Grace.

From the *The Infinite Way* by Joel S. Goldsmith

LOVE

THE EXERCISE OF LOVE

Let brotherly love continue.

Be not forgetful to entertain strangers: for thereby some have entertained angels unawares.

Remember them that are in bonds, as bound with them; and them which suffer adversity, as being yourselves also in the body ...

Let your conversation be without covetousness; and be content with such things as ye have: for he hath said, I will never leave thee, nor forsake thee.

So that we may boldly say, The Lord is my helper, and I will not fear what man shall do unto me.

Remember them which have the rule over you, who have spoken unto you the word of God: whose faith follow, considering the end of their conversation.

Jesus Christ the same yesterday, and today, and forever.

Be not carried about with divers and strange doctrines. For it is a good thing that the heart be established with grace ...

Hebrews, ch. 13

Let every soul be subject unto the higher powers. For there is no power but of God: the powers that be are ordained of God.

Whosoever therefore resisteth the power, resisteth the ordinance of God ...

For rulers are not a terror to good works, but to the evil. Wilt thou then not be afraid of the power? do that which is good, and thou shalt have praise of the same:

For he is the minister of God to thee for good.

Romans, ch. 13

LOVE NOT ONLY IS God but Love is OF God and it manifests itself to us through man.

It might better be said that Love, which is God, manifests itself AS man, for Love is the offspring of God even as man is.

Love, in human experience, seems to be a difficult experience. Looking out upon the world, it would appear that Love is not as prevalent as it might be, that Love is not given and received as it might be. Perhaps we, ourselves, have been partly responsible for this.

Through the ages, we have been taught to be more loving, to be more kind, to be more just. Strangely enough, it does not lie within our power to do that.

At any given moment of our experience, we are as loving and as kind, as merciful and charitable as it is possible to be from that point of consciousness at that moment. For someone to say, "Be MORE loving, be MORE kind, be MORE just," is asking that of us which is impossible.

We and the whole world are giving out love to the full extent of our present capacity.

There IS a way in which we can be more loving, more kind, more just, more charitable, and there IS a way to bring forth more Love from the world, but that way is not by looking to each other FOR it. THAT way lies disappointment.

To ask of each other that we be more loving is NOT the way. Every man and every woman on the face of the earth is being as loving as he knows how to be.

There is only one way to increase that love and that is the way which, if we understood it, would bring peace on earth and good will to all men, and nothing else will. Every HUMAN attempt to bring peace on earth has failed, and failed over a period of thousands of years.

There remains but one way to bring peace on earth and that is through spiritual means. Instead of looking to each other for Love, let us forget each other and let us look to God for Love.

Let us lift our gaze over the heads of our fellow men and REALIZE that since God is Love, ALL Love MUST flow forth FROM God ... NOT FROM MAN ... FROM GOD.

It is true that Love flows THROUGH man, but we only open the avenues of Love through each other by not looking to each other for it but by looking to God for it. The moment we expect Love from each other, we may get hate or indifference. We may find Love today and indifference tomorrow.

The moment we look to each other for justice we may find a measure of it, but we may also find injustice, inequality. There is no way known to bring out justice from a man by expecting it from him. Those who have had experience with law courts can well testify that it isn't even easy to find it on the Bench.

The reason for this is that selfish motives impel most of us just as in our voting at the polls most of us vote according to the way in which we think we will derive the greatest benefit. Rarely do we set aside our personal interests and consider that which would be for the best interests of the Nation. We seldom rise to such heights of unselfishness.

So it is whenever we look for justice, mercy, kindness. We are most apt to find self-interest ... UNTIL we rise above that place where we seek our good from man.

THE SOURCE OF LOVE

ONCE YOU EXPERIENCE the satisfaction of saying, "I shall not fear what man can do to me, nor will I look to man for praise, for honor, for glory, but to God. I will not look to man for kindness, courtesy, consideration, but to God," you will then find that you have touched the SOURCE of Love, the source of Life, the source of Good.

As you continue to focus your attention solely on God, Love begins to flow TO you THROUGH man ... AS man. Not always does Love come through those to whom we are looking for it. Not always does Love come through those from whom we may expect it. However, this becomes of very little importance as we grow in our understanding of Love.

In this life, what everyone wants is Love. We want the opportunity of receiving it. We want the opportunity of expressing it.

At first, we may feel some disappointment at not finding it in those, from those, from whom we have the right to expect it. However, that soon passes and we learn to be grateful for the fact that now our lives are filled with Love, Joy, Peace, Consideration, Cooperation, and we learn to accept it from those whom God gives to us.

It would be possible in just a very few months, at most a very few years, to bring Peace on Earth, if everywhere we were taught not to expect it of man, of nations, of politicians, of government heads, of peace bodies, but to look for it in the ONLY place it can be found ... IN GOD.

Let EVERY soul be subject unto the HIGHER powers. For there is NO power but of God.

Romans 13:1

Let us be subject unto God for our Love, just as in the Infinite Way teaching we subject ourselves to God for our Life. We declare, "God is Life Eternal. God is Infinite. Therefore Life Eternal is Infinite and THAT Life IS my life."

In that same way, we must be subject unto God for Love. We must NOT be subject unto man or unto woman or child. We must be subject unto God ONLY for Love.

Love is of God. Let us therefore look to God for Love and welcome it as it comes to us THROUGH our fellow man. It is in this way that we sometimes entertain angels unawares.

If we are not looking to this individual or to that individual but to God, we will find that the stranger in our midst IS the emissary of God, BRINGING Love to us.

LOVE KNOWS NO LIMITATION

WE CLOSE THE DOOR on Love when we expect it ONLY from our husband or wife or child or parents or neighbor or friend.

We close the door on Love in that way when we pray ONLY for Mother or Father or child or friend or relative.

When we learn to pray for our enemy as we are taught to do in the Master's teachings, when we learn to pray the prayer of forgiveness for all those who offend us, we then find Love coming to us through unexpected avenues and channels.

We, ourselves, limit the amount of Love that ordinarily would be flowing freely to us because we limit it, first of all, to man, and secondly, only to those men and women who comprise our friendly circle.

When we go further afield, when we look not only to friends but even to foes for our Love, through the prayer of forgiveness, we widen that circle, and even more so as we realize God is the fount of ALL Love ... God is the SOURCE of ALL Love.

Therefore, it is to God and ONLY to God that we look for Love. This applies not only to Love as the great word but also to the infinite ramifications of Love.

LOVE IS SUPPLY

SUPPLY IS AN ACTIVITY of Love. We have limited our supply if we have limited it to our positions, our marriages, our inheritances, instead of realizing that supply is actually an activity of Love.

ALL of the supply that ever took place in Scripture came about through the Love of

God for His Creation and through the Love of the prophets, saints and seers of God. THAT Love became manifest as substance.

Therefore, supply IS an activity of Love, and if we limit that to the human avenues of expression, we limit the amount of supply that can come to us. Once we lift our gaze above the human avenues and channels of supply and realize GOD as the source of Love and, therefore, as the source of supply, we begin to open the way for Love to come to us from many new sources.

FORGIVENESS

WE HAVE LOOKED to man for forgiveness for our offenses, our trespasses, our sins. Often, through acts of commission or omission, we have been unloving, unjust, unkind; and sometimes, if possible, we look to those whom we have offended for forgiveness.

In many instances, they have gone so far out of our experience that we have no way of reaching them in order to seek their forgiveness.

Actually, there is no need of our seeking forgiveness of any man. It is well that we apologize, if we have offended. It is well if we ask forgiveness. It is not important whether or not we receive it.

The important point is that we look to GOD for forgiveness ... NOT to man. As long as we look to God for forgiveness, we will be released through man.

Therein lies the miracle ... that even those who, to human sense, would withhold forgiveness, can no longer withhold it when we have sought it in God.

LOVE IS PRACTICAL

IT IS A STRANGE THING but ALL of human experience is a looking to each other for something. ALL of SPIRITUAL experience is a looking to GOD for EVERYTHING.

At first, this is a deep, transitional phase of experience. As we begin the study and practice of The Infinite Way, it is difficult.

It is difficult for the salesman going out to sell to raise himself above the belief that the prospect or the customer has the power to GIVE the order or to WITHHOLD it. From the human standpoint, it would seem that the buyer has the power to give or withhold, but it is not true. We limit the amount of orders we receive by just such a belief. We increase them infinitely when we realize that NO MAN has the power to give or to withhold. ALL POWER IS IN GOD!

14

When we understand this, we can say, "Thank you, Father. Thank you, even that they did not buy." We can say this because it was the Divine Hand that withheld them and kept them from making what might have been a mistake for them.

However, this would in no wise LIMIT our sales.

The same law applies when we go to court. We limit ourselves when we look to judge or to jury for mercy or for justice. These things are not to be found there. There is only a limited human sense of mercy and justice in even the best judge or jury.

However, if we enter the court in the realization that GOD is Love, GOD is Mercy, GOD is Justice, GOD is the seat and source of ALL authority; as we keep our gaze on that One Infinite Being, the source of our Life, the source of our Love, the source of our justice and benevolence, we find it REFLECTED in judge and jury ... sometimes even to their own astonishment.

So it is in every walk of life we have been accustomed to looking to MAN for intelligence. We have even become accustomed to expecting the automobile driver on the road to be a good driver. This is not possible. We can only be good drivers now and then.

However, this is not so in our experience when we realize GOD as the Intelligence of the road; GOD as the Principle, the Law; GOD as the ONLY Driver on the road. In this realization we will experience, not only in our own driving, but in the driving of all those we encounter on the road, Intelligence and Love.

Understand this ... you must not expect good driving from the drivers on the road. You will only find a proportion of it. However, you will find every single driver to be intelligent and loving when you do not expect that of him ... when you expect that ONLY OF GOD.

When you understand GOD as the One Ruling Mind and Intelligence of the Universe, looking to That Mind for Wisdom, Guidance, Direction and Protection, you receive it at the hands of EVERY individual.

LOOKING TO GOD for Life, instead of to bread and to meat, we find Life. We find Life Eternal.

LOOKING TO GOD for Love, instead of to man, we find that Love REFLECTED to us through those we meet.

LOOKING TO GOD for Infinite Wisdom and Intelligence, we find it on the road, in business, in court, WHEREVER WE MAY BE.

It is not difficult to bring about this change if we remember this:

All HUMAN experience is looking to each other.
All SPIRITUAL experience is looking to God.

Remember this as a constant reminder, should you be looking to man, whose breath is in his nostrils; should you be looking to princes, to favoritism, to politics, to man. Look ONLY to God and you will find there the REAL meaning of Love.

Man cannot GIVE Love and man cannot WITHHOLD Love, but the kind of Love that we receive THROUGH man when we look to God for it is the kind of Love that makes us eternally happy, joyous, and it is an unchanging Love. It isn't Love today and indifference or hate tomorrow. It is Love at every level of human experience but an ever expanding Love.

SEEK SPIRITUAL DISCRIMINATION

AS LOVE MANIFESTS ITSELF in our experience, we have a measuring rod for discerning whether it is HUMAN Love or DIVINE Love that we are expressing.

As we live in our homes, in our businesses, in our community and are called upon for expressions of Love in one way or another, we can always ask ourselves, "Do I expect a return?" If we do, it is human Love, finite Love, and a very unsatisfactory Love.

No one ever derives a great joy, even from a gift, even from an expression of Love, when he knows that someone is waiting there for a return.

The Love that gives true satisfaction and joy is the Love we know we didn't deserve and for which no return is expected. It comes straight from the heart with no desire for a return.

That is the guide for us.

As we express our sense of duty to our family, to our friends, to our community, to each other, we must be sure that we are not seeking thanks, appreciation, reward, recognition or praise. Be not afraid, you will have all of these.

The error lies in SEEKING it or EXPECTING it. It is not really Love at all when we express or give it for the purpose or in the expectancy of a return. It is a trade ... like the modern Christmas. It is more of a trade than an expression of Love.

It is possible to perform every family duty without really feeling, "Ah, yes, but in return I am entitled to this." It is not easy because we have been brought up the other way.

However, in turning from the HUMAN sense of experience to the SPIRITUAL (that IS what we are trying to do in our Infinite Way Life—we are trying to emulate the example of The Master; that is the ONLY reason why we are in this work) we start with that idea of letting this Love flow while performing our duties, without looking to the individual for a return, letting the Love express itself as it will.

As we do that and expect our return (whatever return may be necessary) from God, expect our Love from God, we find new relationships on earth.

From the moment you can accept the idea in your mind that LOVE IS OF GOD and the only place to look for it is in and from God and, therefore, whatever of Love you express is God expressing Itself and so you need not take credit for it nor expect a return from it, from that time you enter an entirely new consciousness of life ... one that has different values and one that will explain to you the meaning of Heaven on Earth, because Earth does become transposed into some degree, at least, of Heaven.

Insofar as we can, let us train ourselves and discipline ourselves to LET GOD express Its Love THROUGH us with no idea of return. Look NOT to man, whose breath is in his nostrils, for Love. Rather, expect it as the omnipresent activity of Divine Love.

GRATITUDE

THE MEANING OF GRATITUDE

IT HAS BEEN SAID that "By their works ye shall know them." This truth applies most aptly to Gratitude. Gratitude reflects itself in works. The higher the concept of Gratitude ... the greater the works of the Being reflecting that Gratitude.

The act of expressing Gratitude is in truth the act of recognizing and acknowledging (within yourself) the Source of all your good ... which is God. It is impossible to express Gratitude without expressing Love, as they are both components of God and, therefore, inseparable from God.

Gratitude is akin to Love.

Gratitude, like Love, is God expressing Itself through man as man.

It is impossible to love without expressing some degree of God through your consciousness, and so it is, also, with Gratitude. It is impossible to BE grateful without expressing some degree of God while you are BEING grateful, for Gratitude is of God ... not of man.

Gratitude has a meaning far beyond the word gratitude, itself, or even any idea connected with gratitude. It goes deep into the reality of being.

Gratitude, as it is generally understood, of course, is an outpouring in appreciation for that which we have received. Gratitude SEEMS to express our appreciation for benefits received but, actually, such is not the Truth about Gratitude.

The Truth about Gratitude is this ... you cannot be grateful and you cannot be ungrateful. It does not lie within the power of any individual to be grateful or to express gratitude ... nor does it lie within the power of anyone to withhold gratitude.

GRATITUDE HAS NOTHING TO DO WITH MAN.

Gratitude is one of the many phases or aspects of Love ... and Love is God ... therefore, Gratitude is really a form of God activity or God expression. It is, therefore, true that ONLY God can express Love ... ONLY God can express Gratitude. We can only be the vehicles through which God pours Itself as Love or as Gratitude.

GRATITUDE AS
RELATED TO SUPPLY

GRATITUDE IS CLOSELY AKIN to the subject of supply.

How many times have you heard people say, "Oh! I wish this could be ten times more" or "If I really were expressing my gratitude as I feel it ... this would be a million dollars."

The point here is that gratitude and supply are kindred subjects. If a person had all the supply he wanted, he might believe he would express his gratitude in greater measure. This is not true at all.

Anyone could express his gratitude to the FULLEST, if he understood gratitude in its true sense and he could express his gratitude with SUPPLY to the fullest extent, if he understood the subject of supply.

There is no limit to the Gratitude we can express since Gratitude is of God.

There is no limit to the Love we can express since Love is of God.

There is no limit to the Supply we can express, even in the form of dollars, since Supply is of God.

The main point that we forget is that GOD is individual Being ... GOD is individual You ... and, therefore, you have God-capacity and nothing LESS than God-capacity. You have no capacity of your own. Jesus said,

> *Why callest thou me good? There is none good but one, that is, God.*
>
> Matthew 19:17

We, as individuals, have no personal capacities ... we have no personal limitations ... and we have no personal large amounts in any way, shape, manner or form.

God is Infinite but God is individual Being ... God is your Being ... and that is the point that we miss in our treatments ... in our healing work ... and in our daily living. We continuously set up a selfhood apart from God. Even while in our treatment, we declare, "I and the Father are One. All that the Father hath is mine. I wish this check were bigger." It is not consistent.

If we really want to be consistent in our spiritual approach to life and understand that GOD IS MY INDIVIDUAL BEING and we want to express gratitude (assuming that we only have a dollar bill with which to do it at the moment), we do not apologize for that dollar bill nor do we minimize the dollar bill but we let that dollar bill go forth with all the love that we can feel ... all the joy that we can feel ... sending it forth with no apologies ... no explanations. Here is, at the present moment, your sense of your God-capacity ...

that is ALL. It has no limitation and there is no desire to have it increased because it is the Allness of God coming through at this moment and when you realize that ... that makes room for the Infinite to manifest Itself on greater and greater planes ... greater and greater amounts ... as the unfoldment continues.

Never judge from appearances or you will be limiting your capacity. If you look at your pocketbook, you are judging from appearances. If you even judge of your physical strength, you are judging from appearances ... and you are limiting yourself ... both to the amount of your bank account and to the amount of your physical strength.

By looking beyond the appearance, you realize that God is individual Being ... God is individual You ... the Mind of God is your Mind and, therefore, you are limited in intelligence only to the Wisdom of the Divine Mind ... NOTHING LESS. It is true that much

Wisdom may not seem to be pouring out of you at this particular moment but that has nothing to do with it. You still must not limit your capacity. Your capacity is God-capacity since God is your Mind.

You MUST live ETERNALLY ... since GOD is your LIFE. Judge not by appearances. It is possible you might look into a mirror and find that you look ten or twenty years older than your age. You must not judge by that appearance. You must continue to HOLD to the TRUTH ... that you have only the age of God since God is your Life ... God is ETERNALLY your Life ... since, before Abraham was, God is your Life and God will be your Life unto the end of the world. Therefore, your Life can know no age ... no limitation.

Since GOD is the Substance of your Being ... your supply must be Infinite. There is no need to look in your pocketbook or your bank account to see how closely you are approximating that in demonstration. Judge NOT by appearances ... STAND ON THE TRUTH THAT ... since God is the Substance of your Being, God is Infinite, your Substance is likewise Infinite.

Then, if you spend one dollar, you will think of it as THAT Infinity pouring forth as THAT dollar ... but STILL the Infinity. That makes room for it to become two or twenty or two hundred dollars ... but not by limiting ... not by judging ... but by understanding that GOD IS my Substance ... God is Infinite, therefore, my Substance and my Supply are Infinite. Thus, in paying out even one dollar you are giving out Infinity.

GRATITUDE AS RELATED TO LOVE

LOVE HAS TO DO with Gratitude. Love has to do with Supply. Love has to do with caring and protecting. Statements of Truth with reference to Love may also be applied to Gratitude as both are attributes of God, the same as Life, Peace, Joy, Harmony, etc.

How much Love can we express? How foolish it is to say, "I wish I could be more loving" or "I would like to be more loving." It is ridiculous. You cannot be MORE loving ... you cannot be LESS loving ... since God is the ONLY loving you possess.

God is Infinite ... therefore, you possess INFINITE Love, and INFINITE Love is expressed FROM you and TO you.

This is the point that wrecks most of our lives: We believe that there are those who could GIVE us more love and we believe that there are those who are WITHHOLDING love from us. This is a fatal error.

No one can give us any more love than they are giving, and no one has the power to withhold love.

LOVE is GOD EXPRESSING Itself!

God cannot express Itself finitely. God cannot express Itself in a limited form or a limited way or in a limited amount. The error has been that you are looking to a person for Love, and a person does not HAVE Love to GIVE. Love is of God. In fact, Love IS God. In fact, God IS Love.

If you look to a person for love, you will find often, in place of love ... hate ... or you will find a love that TURNS to hate. The error, then, is NOT the other person's ... the error is NOT on the part of those who WITHHOLD love ... or SEEM to withhold. The error is on OUR part in EXPECTING love from a person ... or in CONDEMNING him for WITHHOLDING love. He cannot withhold what is not his ... he cannot give what is not his.

Love is of God. The moment we turn our thought FROM the idea that a PERSON can give or withhold love ... we FIND love pouring itself out to us in Infinite abundance ... although not always from those from whom we have been expecting it ... or not always from those from whom we have the right to expect it.

It does not lie within our ability to change people in their demonstration. ALL we can change is OUR demonstration.

If we are not receiving enough love in the world, let us stop looking to people for it and look to God for it. It will appear, though not always through the person from whom you expect it. That is one of the things that we must learn ... that it is not up to us to DETERMINE from what direction Love is to come ... it MUST come from God.

LOOK NOT TO MAN

IT IS NOT UP TO US to determine from what direction Gratitude is to come ... it MUST come from God.

The individual who has learned the Wisdom of GOD as Love, looks to God to express Itself even in what we call gratitude ... sharing. As we keep our vision on God as the source of our supply ... on God even as the source of the gratitude that must come to us ... Gratitude COMES ... not always from those who SHOULD be giving the most of it ... but it COMES.

Who are we to judge who the channel should be ... or the vehicle ... or the avenue ... today or tomorrow? Sufficient for us IF we are EXPERIENCING the Love of God made manifest as Gratitude ... the Love of God made manifest as sharing ... cooperation ... joy ... the Love of God made manifest as Love ... without our trying to DETERMINE ... who? ... when? ... or how much?

Healing work will be very simple ONCE you begin to realize that God is individual Being and NO person has the capacity to BE sick. No person has the capacity to be sick ... or to be well. God is the ONE Divine Life ... the ONLY Life ... and It is individual Life ... YOUR Life ... and because It is God ... It has no capacity to be sick. It has no capacity to be weak.

Therefore, as you learn to keep your vision on GOD as individual Being ... as YOUR

Being ... you will find NOTHING in your Being "... that defileth ... or maketh a lie." (Revelation 21:27)

AGAIN, we must not judge by appearances. At this present moment, ALL of us (in appearance) are showing forth some phase of discord ... inharmony ... ill health ... lack. The REASON is that we have not FULLY realized God as individual Being. We STILL have a selfhood apart from God.

As long as we look to someone outside of ourselves for love ... gratitude ... supply ... we have not REALIZED that God is our own individual Being. Therefore, we have no right to look OUT THERE for love ... gratitude ... or supply. We must ONLY look to God ... THE God of our own Being ... NOT OUT THERE ... NOT in our homes ... only to the God of our own Being. THEN ... let it come through whom it will ... or from whatever direction it will.

If we look to the God of another Being ... we look amiss. We should look to the God of our OWN Being. GOD is individual Being ... GOD is YOUR individual Being. Therefore, God is pouring Its Love TO you ... THROUGH you ... AS you ... OUT into the world. This is true of EVERY individual.

As long as you have God (and the Kingdom of God is WITHIN YOU) ... as long as you have the ENTIRE Kingdom of God within YOU, pouring Itself forth as Love ... Joy ... Companionship ... Supply ... Gratitude ... WHY should you be looking out there for it? As long as you do not look out there for it, SOMEBODY out there ... or MANY bodies ... WILL be the vehicles or avenues bringing it to your door. LOOKING OUT THERE for it is the error.

GOD is individual Being. GOD is YOUR individual Being. It is RIGHT to ask the practitioner or the teacher for help ... but it is also right to understand that THAT help is coming from the God of your OWN Being ... from the Kingdom of God within YOU.

Every experience to you in your life is YOUR OWN CONSCIOUSNESS of Truth unfolding ... whether it comes to you as Love ... whether it comes to you as Supply ... or Gratitude ... or Success ... or Health. Regardless of whom it SEEMS to come through ... it may be husband or wife, parent or child, or a friend ... it is YOUR OWN CONSCIOUSNESS of TRUTH unfolding.

The moment YOU realize God as individual Being ... the moment you realize God as YOUR individual Being ... the Infinity of Good MUST unfold from WITHIN YOU ... THROUGH YOU ... TO the world ... nothing

LESS than Infinity. Then you never have to apologize, because you never lack ... you never have an insufficiency ... whether it is of strength ... whether it is of healing power ... whether it is of understanding ... whether it is of gratitude ... or whether it is of supply.

You cannot have an insufficiency of any kind IF your Source is God ... THAT makes the Source of it Infinite. When you personalize it and set up a selfhood apart from God ... then ... when you are called on to feed four thousand, five thousand and women and children, too ... you cannot do it. You explain that you do not have that many farms or storehouses or barns ... you do not have that many bonds or bank accounts. You have set up this personal selfhood and expect it to meet the demands that are made upon you. Naturally, you fail to meet the need.

You might just as well be a practitioner and have a hundred people come to you with various diseases and you respond by saying, "Oh ... Oh ... I couldn't possibly heal all these people of all these diseases." Certainly, you could not ... of yourself. You have nothing to do it with ... BUT ... in the understanding of God as the REAL Law of Being, you have the Capacity of God to do the healing and you can heal multitudes.

No one knows what demands may be made upon them tomorrow or in the near future. You may be called upon to feed many hundreds of people or you may be called upon to heal many thousands of people and you wonder where the supply or the healing is going to come from. It is going to come from God ... THROUGH YOU ... once you realize that God IS your individual Being and EVERY demand made upon you can be fulfilled.

NO demand can EVER be made upon you for Love, Joy, Gratitude or Supply that you cannot fulfill, since it is not of you ... it is of God. If necessary, there will be a multiplication of loaves and fishes but YOU won't multiply them any more than Jesus did. GOD WILL DO THE WORK.

Jesus looked up to the Father and the loaves and the fishes were multiplied. In other words, Jesus recognized, "I can of my own self do nothing but the Father WITHIN ME multiplies the loaves and fishes ... and even produces gold in the fishes' mouths."

When you realize God to be your CAPACITY, you have INFINITE capacity. Then, despite appearances, never apologize ... never explain ... just hold to the Truth of Being. Never apologize for a limitation. Never apologize for a lack of demonstration.

RECOGNITION AND ACKNOWLEDGMENT

NO ONE HAS THE RIGHT ... at this particular stage of unfoldment ... to expect any of us to be the FULL Christ-head. Anyone of us may achieve it today or tomorrow ... and there may be some among us who HAVE achieved it ... but they are not known to the public at large. However, we may be assured of this ... that we HAVE achieved a wonderful measure of it in Truth work and in our understanding ... and ... regardless of what inharmony or discord presents itself today, we have a WONDERFUL thing with which to meet it.

What is that WONDERFUL THING? The REALIZATION of GOD as individual BEING.

As we continue to progress in that unfoldment and gain greater and greater realizations of it, we will show forth greater demonstrations of it ... ONLY, however, IF we can begin with a Principle. We MUST know WHAT the Principle is ... and the Principle begins with the word GOD ... NOT God separate and apart from you ... NOT you separate and apart from God ... but GOD as YOUR individual BEING ... the Divine Mind as your individual Mind ... the one Infinite Life as your individual Life ... the one Divine Substance as the Substance even of your body ... of your being ... of your business ... of ALL that concerns YOU.

THAT understanding of ONENESS, accepted even intellectually, BEGINS to be the foundation of the spiritual apprehension of the idea ... and it is the SPIRITUAL DISCERNMENT that results in demonstration.

Often we NEED this letter ... this correct letter of Truth ... for our foundation. We must KNOW what the Principle is that we are trying to demonstrate ... and the Principle IS God ... as your individual Being ... God, as your Capacity ... God, as the amount of ALL that concerns you ... God, as the amount of your supply ... God, as the amount of your gratitude ... God, as the amount of your love.

Why should you be limited in expressing love if it is not you expressing at all but rather God expressing Itself—?

Why should love be limited in its expression to you if you are looking to God to express Itself as Love?

As long as you keep looking to God to express Itself as Love, you MUST receive the FULL MEASURE of God-Love. When you limit it to a person's capacity to express love ... or when you limit your supply to the amount of a person's bank account ... you are lost. REALIZE THIS!

In ALL relationships, do not look to each other as though THAT person could give or withhold. It is of the utmost importance that we realize, at all times, that we are not looking to a person but to the Christ of his Being and of our Being.

It is for this reason that at some period in our study we must make a CONSCIOUS exercise along this line (call it a discipline, if you will): at some period we must agree that EVERYONE we meet in the course of the day is Christ. As we get up in the morning and greet members of our family, do not dwell on personalities by liking this one and disliking that one and finding fault with another one. Rather, secretly, inwardly, greet each one as The Christ.

As we leave home and go to the market or the stores or business, all whom we meet we must CONSCIOUSLY recognize as The Christ. The Christ of you greets the Christ of them. The Christ of you loves the Christ of them. The Christ of them loves the Christ of you. In our Christhood we are One. We are not looking at appearances now. We are not thinking of male or female. We are not thinking of what we must give or what we shall receive. We are thinking only of TRUE IDENTITY.

Are we expecting even COURTESY from store people? We have no right to, because they do not have it to give ... they do not have it to withhold. Only The Christ expresses Itself AS Courtesy. Therefore, we should look to The Christ of each one, and not to the outer. Otherwise, it would be the same as if we were looking at a cluster of electric lights and expecting the light from the bulbs.

The light is not there at all. The light is an emanation of the electricity.

If we were to limit ourselves by looking to the bulb for light, sooner or later we would be disappointed, as the bulb would burn out and we would be without light ... BUT, as long as we are looking to the electricity, we will have light, even if we have to produce a new bulb.

So it is with us. If we are looking to GOD for Love, we will always have it ... BUT ... if we are looking to PERSONS for love, they may burn out or they may turn to hate ... indifference ... ingratitude.

If we are looking to GOD, whatever happens out here in this scene (the visible world) will make no difference. This one may get washed away ... that one may turn away ... Judas will betray ... Peter will deny ... Thomas will doubt ... BUT IT WILL MAKE NO DIFFERENCE.

We expected nothing of Judas ... we expected nothing of Peter ... we expected nothing of Thomas. ALL we expected was of GOD.

What happens to Judas? He commits suicide ... and a twelfth one is appointed to take his place. The work goes right on. The love goes right on. The ministry goes right on because the Minister ... God ... is there. What happens to Judas? Who cares?

What happens to those who betray ... slander ... defame ... or are ungrateful? Who cares? They are living in accord with the law:

Be not deceived; God is not mocked: for whatsoever a man soweth, that shall he also reap.

Galatians 6:7

That is not your demonstration ... it is their demonstration.

AS WE SOW

WE, TOO, ARE LIVING in accord with the law of "As we sow, so shall we reap."

IF WE SOW to GOD AS the source of our good, we will reap infinite, eternal good ... regardless of what happens to all the people in our experience.

Scripture says, "When my father and my mother forsake me, then the Lord will take me up." (Psalm 27:10)

It is possible for fathers and mothers to forsake children and it is possible for children to forsake parents, and so we have no right to look to father or mother or children. OUR looking ... OUR sowing should ALWAYS be to God.

If you sow to the Spirit you will reap Spiritual Good, and if you sow to the flesh you will reap corruption.

If you sow, if you expect your good from man, whose breath is in his nostrils, sooner or later you must meet with Judas ... with doubting Thomas ... with the denying Peter. As a matter of fact, even if you do not have that experience, you will probably have all twelve disciples go to sleep on you. It is not always downright evil that betrays us. It can be just something like that ... going to sleep on the job.

When we look to person, place or thing for gratitude ... for supply ... for love ... for companionship ... anything that happened to Jesus through his disciples can happen to us through those to whom we look. That is the lesson Jesus gave us through the disciples. Each served his purpose in proportion to his capacity but not one of them endured.

However, Jesus' principle of Life eternal endured because even without the twelve disciples, He still walked out of the tomb and walked out in His own body ... the same body that had been wounded. His Principle did not betray Him ... nor did His Principle forsake Him. Even if it were true that He had spoken those words, "Why hast Thou forsaken me?" we know that was merely a temporary weakness caused by His disappointment at the failure of all His disciples. He quickly realized, however, that His Principle had not forsaken Him because He walked out of the tomb.

So it is with us. God is individual Being, and since God is Love ... Love is Infinite in Being. Therefore, you can know nothing less than an infinity of Love.

God is Mind ... But God is Divine Mind. Therefore, you can know nothing less than an infinity of Wisdom ... Intelligence ... Guidance ... Direction.

God is Substance. Therefore, you can know nothing less than Infinite Substance ... and so on through all the synonyms.

Once you grasp the idea of God as individual Being, you will solve all the problems of so-called human existence. Then you will find that Gratitude is not something that you can give or withhold. It is something that God expresses through you. When you try to limit it or even to increase it, you are getting in the way of God's activity.

CORRECT YOUR CONCEPTS

NOW WE COME to the ultimate of this subject which began with just Gratitude. Let us consider the point that, when Jesus walked out of the tomb, it was with the same body that had been crucified ... in which the wounds were still apparent.

The moment you understand God as individual Being ... God as the Substance of all form ... you will understand that your body is Spiritual and that your body is just as Infinite and just as Eternal as your Gratitude ... as your Supply ... as your Love. Your body does not differ from your love. Your body does not differ from your supply or your gratitude or your benevolence or your cooperation or your sharing or your wisdom. Your body is as infinite and as eternal as God since God is the Substance thereof. God is the Substance of which your body is formed.

Therefore, for one reason or another, through ignorance or desire, should you experience what we know as death or transition or passing on (it makes no difference what name you use ... a rose, by any other name, is just as sweet) you will find just what Jesus demonstrated ... that you have not left a body here for burial or for cremation ... you have taken your body with you ... and all its wounds with it too. The form of your body will change in proportion to your ascending consciousness of Truth.

Jesus knew that His body was eternal. He knew that it was immortal. Understanding this, He knew that the crucifixion could not destroy His Life or His Body. Jesus' wisdom was greater than the understanding of those who believe that Life is Spirit ... Life is God ... Life is Eternal ... but that Life inhabits a material body.

Jesus knew that there was only one Creator and that Creator was God (or Spirit) and, therefore, It could not create a material body. He also knew the Book of Genesis. If God did not create it ... it was not made. So, if God did not create a material body ... there is no material body. If God is Infinite Spirit and made this world in Its own image and likeness, then the body that God made must be Spirit ... it must be spiritual ... it must partake of the nature and character of Spirit.

Had Jesus returned from the tomb without that body, He would not have proven Immortality. He would not have proven God as the Substance of all form ... as the Creator of the Universe out of Its own Being. Since God is individual Being and God is your Mind and your Life ... God is the Substance of your body, and your body is as Infinite and Eternal and Omnipresent as the Body of God ... as the Substance or Life of God.

The moment you accept that fact intellectually, you begin ultimately to discern it spiritually and then you will demonstrate that the body has no power to age ... lose its vitality ... or die. Your body becomes as immortal as your own idea of Truth. If you acknowledge, "I am the Truth," you must also acknowledge, "My body is the Body of the Truth."

Scripture says your body is the Temple of God:

> *What? Know ye not that your body is the temple of the Holy Ghost which is in you, which ye have of God, and ye are not your own?*
>
> 1 Corinthians 6:19

We are not judging by appearances ... we are recognizing Truth as it is. The Truth is that God is The Substance of which this world was formed. Whether the world appears as earth, trees, sky, sun, moon, stars, or whether it appears as your body, it still is of the Substance and of the Activity of God, and it is Infinite ... Immortal ... Eternal ... Omnipresent.

If God cannot change, neither can the body change. If God cannot age, neither can God, appearing as Body, age. Therefore, the body IS immortal and eternal and unless you understand that from the resurrection of the Master, you have lost the main point. There are reasons why it is necessary that we understand this.

It is senseless for us to go on as Infinite Way students ... claiming to know something and to have something ... and yet continue being just as sick as other people, just as old as other people and just as decrepit as other people.

It is simply nonsensical to be a student of The Infinite Way and to CLAIM an understanding and demonstration of Truth, and yet to keep on experiencing the same diseases, the same accidents and the same everything else that other people have.

We are told to come out and be separate and we MUST come out and be separate ... NOT in just claiming that we have demonstrated the fullness of the Christ-head ... NO ... but at least in claiming a progressive unfoldment of Christhood. It is only by constant application of effort toward the goal that we can show forth a little more of the Christ from year to year ... not only in our loving kindness or understanding to each other ... not only in our greater charity to each other ... but also in our physical appearance.

Why should we claim that each year we are more loving ... more kind ... more just ... and yet insist that each year we are older ... weaker? It is not consistent.

It IS necessary that, through our Infinite Way study, we understand God as Love and, therefore, that we MUST show forth more love ... more justice ... more kindness ... more peace toward each other. This is true ... but ... let us not stop there and separate the body from our spiritual demonstration. Let us bring the body into line WITH our spiritual demonstration and let us show forth more of the God-body each year. Let us show forth a higher concept of the real body so that we can bring our whole demonstration into line.

This point naturally follows: There is not a spiritual universe and a material universe. There is not something good in the world and something bad in the world. There is only ONE Power and there is only ONE Presence and It is ALL Good.

What we are called upon to do is change our concepts ... not change the world. You cannot change your body ... even by dying ... but you can change the APPEARANCE of your body by changing your concept OF your body. Your body cannot change. It is Spiritual ... Infinite ... Eternal ... Harmonious ... Perfect.

Going around affirming this statement won't help you one bit ... and it won't make it so ... IT IS ALREADY SO. You must come into the realization of it THROUGH knowing WHY it is true.

God is individual Being. Therefore, God must be the Substance of individual Being and Body. God is the very Activity of your Body. How can it be less Active tomorrow than today or yesterday ... if God is the Activity of It?

If God is the Activity of your Supply, how can your supply be greater one day than another? The fluctuations in supply are merely the result of the belief that you have a supply of your own which can go up and down.

The fluctuations in the health and strength of the body come only from the belief that we have a health or a body of our own ... instead of realizing GOD as individual Being ... GOD as the Substance of Being and of Body ... and THEN realizing that the ONLY capacity we have is God-capacity. This capacity is not only a God-capacity for expressing Gratitude but it is also a God-capacity for expressing Youth ... Health ... Vitality ... Strength ... Wisdom ... and all the other qualities of God.

You must come to the realization that this is NOT a partly spiritual universe and partly material universe.

You must come to the realization that this universe is wholly spiritual and that there is no evil in it ... therefore, it is useless to try to fight error or fight evil. Rather, agree with your adversary by saying, "All right ... you may appear to be so but I am not going to fight it. I take my stand that God IS individual Being and, therefore, NOTHING can enter individual Being that defileth or maketh a lie."

If, temporarily, there is an appearance to the contrary, forget the appearance ... overlook it ... disregard it ... and HOLD STEADFAST to the Truth that God IS individual Being. You have no life apart from God ... no mind ... no soul ... no body ... no CAPACITY apart from God. God is the Infinite Capacity of your Being and of your Body.

Meditate on that.

Nothing you can do or think can MAKE this true. It IS true ... and it is not MADE true by any effort.

Not by might, nor by power, but by my spirit, saith the Lord of hosts.

Zechariah 4:6

As we open our consciousness to let GOD reveal this to us, instead of trying to argue it out or reason it out or find reasons why it cannot be or is not, let us forget that battle (the physical battle ... or the mental battle) and realize this:

WHATEVER IS TRUE WILL REVEAL ITSELF TO YOU FROM WITHIN YOUR OWN BEING IF YOU WILL JUST OPEN YOUR CONSCIOUSNESS TO IT.

If there were a word not true in this, you would be informed of that, too.

Do NOT make a MENTAL effort to understand all this. It is far too deep for the mind to grasp. It is far too high for any HUMAN intellect to agree with. It is too high spiritually. You will only be able to understand it through the Soul faculties ... through your spiritual consciousness.

Therefore, open your mind in this wise ... that whatever Truth IS, must reveal Itself to you ... not by might ... not by power ... but by "MY SPIRIT" ... for so saith the Lord.

ALOHA

Made in United States
North Haven, CT
23 December 2022

30036395R00046